Harlec

Arnold Taylor CBE, DLitt, FBA

Introduction

ân, the son of Llŷr, was the crowned king of
d exalted with the crown of London. And one
was at Harlech in Ardudwy in his court. And
ing upon the rock of Harlech, above the sea ...'

A New Translation, by T. P. Ellis and John Lloyd, 2 vols

with the mountains
the sea not far from
uation has made it
in the British Isles.
ed natural setting;
lech is also unrivalled.
of genius. The master
natural strength
of the site to the accommodation and defence
requirements of his patron has produced a building
that combines a marvellous sense of power with
great beauty of line and form. Now some seven
centuries old, Harlech was completed in all essentials
from ground to battlements in a mere seven years.
It is a strikingly successful realization of a single design
concept, perfectly attuned both to its purpose and
its natural surroundings.

This guidebook sets out firstly to explain when
and why the castle came to be built, who its architect
and builders were, and how the work of building was
carried out. Secondly, the castle's subsequent history
is traced through the centuries, and some of the
episodes of national significance in which it had a
part to play are recalled. Finally, there is a tour of
the castle buildings, outlining the plan and layout
of the stronghold, and explaining the purpose of the
walls and towers and the interior buildings. All the
principal features are indicated, and details of interest

pointed out. In short, the purpose of the tour
is to make the castle tell its own story. To the
interested visitor, a castle like Harlech is constantly
saying, 'if you want to know about me, look carefully
at me and I will tell you'. For most of us, buildings
speak in a language difficult to understand without
help. Part of the guidebook's role is to translate
and interpret, to recall the forgotten and help the
castle come alive again.

*Opposite: The spectacular
position of the castle, with the
mountains of Snowdonia beyond,
is best appreciated from a rocky
knoll to the south of the town.
The subject of countless pictures,
this view has made Harlech one
of the most familiar strongholds
in the British Isles.*

*The great seal of King Edward I
(1272–1307), the builder of
Harlech Castle (Public Record
Office).*

A History of Harlech Castle

The Building of the Castle: 1283–89

Harlech is one of a group of great new castles built in or on the borders of north Wales for King Edward I (1272–1307) of England in the last quarter of the thirteenth century. There were fourteen of them, with Flint, Rhuddlan, Ruthin, Hope, Builth and Aberystwyth begun in 1277; Conwy, Harlech and Caernarfon, which were begun in that order between March and June 1283; Denbigh, Hawarden, Holt and Chirk which were constructed after 1284; and Beaumaris, the last of the group, begun in 1295. To complete the list of Edwardian castle works in north Wales, one has also to include the repair and rebuilding — from 1283 onwards — of Dolwyddelan, Criccieth and Castell y Bere, war-damaged strongholds of the former Welsh princes.

Neither history nor archaeology furnish any evidence to suggest that Harlech itself had formerly had a castle of the princes. In Welsh mythology, however, the place is associated inseparably and for ever with the legend of Branwen, the daughter of Llŷr, the opening lines of which (p. 3) are the proper prologue to the story that follows.

In the month of May 1283, Harlech emerges from the realms of folk-tale and myth into the light of recorded fact. Six months earlier, in December 1282, Llywelyn ap Gruffudd, the first and last Welsh prince of all Wales, had been killed near Builth. In January, the castle of Dolwyddelan in Snowdonia had fallen to the English after a hard-pressed siege. In April, the Welsh garrison at the castle of Bere in the southern folds of Cader Idris also surrendered after a ten-day siege.

Dolwyddelan's capture opened the way for King Edward's northern force to advance down the Conwy valley. Building of the new castle and walled town, which still stand near the river's mouth today,

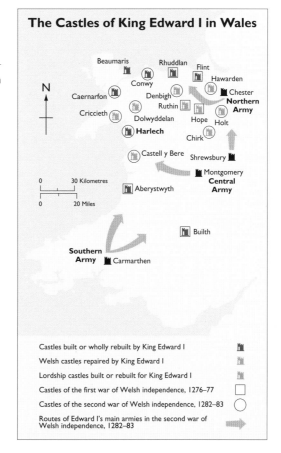

The Castles of King Edward I in Wales

N

Beaumaris
Rhuddlan
Flint
Conwy
Hawarden
Caernarfon
Denbigh
Chester
Criccieth
Ruthin
Northern Army
Dolwyddelan
Hope
Holt
Harlech
Chirk
Castell y Bere
Shrewsbury
Montgomery
Central Army
Aberystwyth

0   30 Kilometres

0   20 Miles

Builth

Southern Army
Carmarthen

Castles built or wholly rebuilt by King Edward I
Welsh castles repaired by King Edward I
Lordship castles built or rebuilt for King Edward I
Castles of the first war of Welsh independence, 1276–77
Castles of the second war of Welsh independence, 1282–83
Routes of Edward I's main armies in the second war of Welsh independence, 1282–83

Opposite: The construction of Harlech Castle was begun in the spring of 1283 and building was virtually complete by 1289. In this fifteenth-century French manuscript illumination, a king is shown seated with his master mason providing a building report. The round tower under construction is decked with spiral, or helicoidal, scaffolding. Evidence survives in several towers to demonstrate that this same technique was employed at Harlech (British Library, Royal Ms. 15 D III, f. 15v).

In December 1282, Llywelyn ap Gruffudd — the first and last Welsh prince of all Wales — was killed in or after a substantial skirmish a few miles from Builth in Powys. This manuscript depiction of the event may reflect the English bias of the source (British Library, Cotton Nero Ms. D II, f. 182).

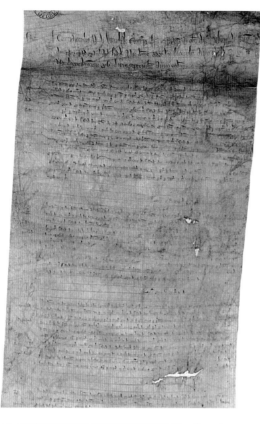

was commenced in March. A month later, the elimination of Castell y Bere cleared the way for the central force of 560 infantry under King Edward's Savoyard lieutenant, Sir Otto de Grandison (1238–1328), to march up through the Welsh districts of Meirionydd and Ardudwy to Harlech. Work on the new castle was begun immediately. Between 14 and 20 May, two panniers containing £100 in hard cash were sent under guard from the Cistercian abbey of Cymer to the site chosen for the new castle 'for the works there'. And a month later we read of twenty stonemasons and quarriers being sent off from the newly established base at Conwy to Harlech, with a packhorse to carry their tools on the two-day journey across the mountains. In July, another fifteen masons and a squad of carpenters followed on the same journey. Three years later, with the work at its height in the summer of 1286, nearly 950 men were employed — 227 masons, 115 quarriers, 30 smiths, 22 carpenters and as many as 546 labourers and minor workmen.

The overall plan of the castle was determined at the very outset of the works. Thereafter, by combining the evidence of our eyes with what we can learn from surviving records, we can see by

what stages the construction of the stronghold gradually moved forward to completion.

The earliest stage was achieved in the first few building seasons, and was probably completed before construction work stopped for the winter of 1283–84. Evidently, this phase saw the erection of the main inner curtain wall of the castle. But it was only raised to such a height and thickness as would provide — in the shortest possible time — a strong defensible enclosure within which the garrison and workforce could be accommodated as further building proceeded. Looking carefully, especially at the outside of the north and south curtains, you will see a horizontal break-line in the masonry at a height of about 15 feet (4.5m) from the ground. The build of the stonework above this line differs from that below. Evidence of a similar change can also be detected on the two eastern corner towers. The north, south and west curtains also show evidence, up to the same height, of a vertical break. Each of these sections of wall was at first built only to about two-thirds of its ultimate thickness. In the case of the north and south curtains, it is the outer face which is the earlier and thicker, whereas on the west curtain it is the inner side of the wall. A works account survives which actually mentions the final thickening and heightening of the walls as having been completed in 1289.

The 1284 and 1285 building seasons are likely to have seen substantial progress with the construction of the lower parts of the great gatehouse, built as it was astride the line of the eastern curtain. At the same time, headway was probably also made on the concentric outer curtain wall, with its turreted gateways to the east and to the north, and the great corbelled latrine chute projecting out over the rock-cut ditch to the south. A record survives of a major payment being made for work during the 1285 season on the cutting of this ditch. From another record, it is clear that by the end of the same year certain rooms in the gatehouse were being prepared for occupation. They were intended for the newly-appointed constable of the castle, Sir John de Bonvillars (d. 1287).

Building expenditure at Harlech rose to a peak of nearly £240 a month over the fourteen months from September 1286 to November 1287. It was to average rather less than half this figure over the two succeeding years. A fragmentary account belonging

Master James of St George

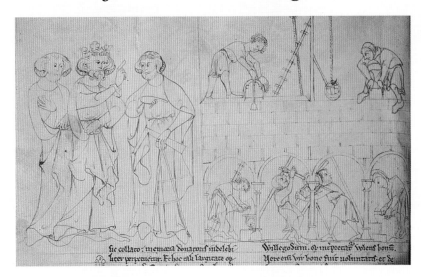

sic collaco : memoria donaronf indelebi   Willegodum. q̃ mcipiecac̃ uolenf bonꝰ.
licce ꝑpetuecur. Ec hoc cali lauaicace op   Here ent̃ ʋir bone fuic uoluncacif. ec de

Like the other north Wales Crown castles that were its contemporaries, Harlech's construction was directed by the brilliant James of St George. Born about 1235, James was a highly-paid master mason and military engineer who came to Wales from distant Savoy in 1278. He had earlier worked as the chief household architect for two of the counts of Savoy: Peter II (1263–68), and Philip (1268–85). King Edward I secured his services by arrangement with Count Philip, and brought him to Wales to superintend his new castle-building programme.

In July 1290 the king appointed him constable of Harlech, a fitting honour which for the next three years Master James held in conjunction with his post as master of the works. He resided with his wife, Ambrosia, in all probability in the great gatehouse which stands to this day as witness to his creative skill. In 1295, James was granted a life pension, together with the manor of Mostyn in north-east Wales. In May 1309 the manor was described as 'late of Master James of St George, deceased'.

In this mid-thirteenth-century manuscript illumination, a king is seen directing his master mason, with construction work underway in the background. Harlech's designer and master mason was the brilliant military engineer, James of St George. Master James served as constable of Harlech from 1290 to 1293 (British Library, Cotton Nero Ms. D I, f. 23 v).

Chillon, Switzerland, where Master James may have been at work for Count Peter II of Savoy in 1266-67 (Peter Humphries).

A reconstruction of Harlech Castle as it may have appeared about 1325. The main components of the inner and outer wards as well as the water gate, seen in the foreground of this view from the north-west, were complete by 1289. To the left of the water gate, the wall encircling the base of the castle rock to the north was added about 1295. Outside the great gatehouse, the two bridge towers spanning the castle ditch were further additions of 1323–24 (Illustration by Terry Ball, 1985; with modifications, 1996).

to the end of the year 1289 shows that by then the building of the castle was virtually finished. The two western towers — 'the towers towards the sea' — had been added in a single operation, and their turrets and those of the gatehouse all stood complete to their battlements. The main curtains had also been thickened and, with the eastern corner towers, carried up to their full height. The long sloping path up from the water gate — 'the way from the sea' — had already been constructed, together with the wall closing off the south-west end of the ditch and the corresponding wall running out to the edge of the rock from the mantelet below

the north-west tower. Inside the castle ward, the walls of the hall, the chapel, the pantry and kitchen had all been built.

The composition of the permanent garrison had been established in 1284. It was to comprise a constable, 'together with 30 fencible men of whom 10 shall be crossbowmen', one chaplain, an artiller, a smith, a carpenter and a mason, 'and from the others shall be made janitors, watchmen, and other necessary officers'. By the end of the decade, the castle whose defence and maintenance was entrusted to them thus stood to all intents and purposes complete.

The two stumps of masonry in the ditch — in front of the modern timber stairs — indicate the position of two stone towers and a bridge that were added in 1323–24 to strengthen the eastern approach to the castle.

Secondary Works

Harlech's viability was first put to the test at the time of Madog ap Llywelyn's rising in 1294–95. During this widespread national revolt, the castle was entirely cut off by land. Indeed, the same was true of Criccieth, the Welsh castle across the bay which had been occupied and repaired by the English since the war of 1282–83. But the coastal position of the two strongholds enabled them to be supplied and victualled from Ireland by sea, and both held out. As soon as the war was over, steps were taken to strengthen one remaining area of potential weakness at Harlech. Although the defended 'way from the sea' had already been constructed up the flank of the western precipice, the castle rock to the north had been left to rely on the natural protection of the deep ravine and waterfall bounding it on that side. Orders were now given for the rock to be enclosed with a wall of stone and lime, and a new tower was built over or near the water gate.

More than a quarter of a century later, in 1323–24, the castle was further strengthened. Harlech had probably become a main base for the forces led by Sir Gruffudd Llwyd, sheriff of Merioneth, in support of King Edward II (1307–27) against the Mortimers. It was at this time that the bridge approach from the east was strongly fortified with the erection of two towers. Constructed in line, one 60 feet (18m) the other 40 feet (12m) high, the towers sprang from the base of the ditch in front of the entrance gateway. Their stumps can be seen beside and below the modern approach path and stairway. A sixteenth-century description of the castle shows that in the centre — between the two towers — there was a stone-arched bridge, with a drawbridge at either end.

Harlech seems to have been involved in little activity during the remainder of the fourteenth century, but an awareness of its strategic importance is perhaps indicated by the fact that for forty years, from 1332 to 1372, the constableship was in the hands of Sir Walter Manny, one of the ablest soldiers to serve King Edward III (1327–77), and one of the most prominent figures of the reign.

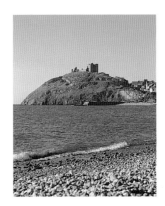

Like Harlech, Criccieth Castle was cut off by land during the Welsh revolt of 1294–95, but the coastal position of both fortresses allowed them to be supplied from Ireland by sea.

Harlech fell to the forces of Owain Glyn Dŵr late in 1404, and it was held by the Welsh for the next four years. The arms of Glyn Dŵr appear on this harness decoration found at the castle in 1923 (National Museum of Wales).

Harlech and Owain Glyn Dŵr

Harlech Castle played a key role in the events and incidents that marked the great Welsh uprising of about 1400 to 1414. Led by the charismatic Owain Glyn Dŵr, the revolt was to prove the last major Welsh rebellion against English rule. By 1403, the scale of the revolt had become truly national. In the north and west, the castles at Aberystwyth, Beaumaris, Caernarfon and Harlech had become isolated outposts of English authority. An inventory of military supplies at Harlech taken in June of that year shows just how difficult it was for the garrison to mount an effective defence of the stronghold. There were just three shields, eight basinets, six lances (four lacking heads), ten pairs of less than useful gloves, four guns, and various stocks of iron and lead.

After long sieges, Harlech and Aberystwyth finally fell into Welsh hands, probably in the closing months of 1404. Their control gave Owain unfettered authority in central Wales. Harlech became the residence of his court and his family, and with Machynlleth it was one of two places to which he summoned parliaments of his supporters. There is a tradition that at one of these, and Harlech is perhaps the more likely, he was formally crowned as prince of Wales in the presence of envoys from Scotland, France and Spain.

The occupation of Harlech by a Welsh garrison loyal to Owain Glyn Dŵr came to an end after a long siege in 1408–09. The English force was led by Prince Harry of Monmouth, later King Henry V (1413–22). The young prince is depicted in this manuscript illumination (British Library, Arundel Ms. 38, f. 37).

In 1408–09, Harlech was again under siege; this time a Welsh garrison suffered under persistent cannonading. One of the massive cannon employed by the attacking English force bore the name 'the king's daughter'; we have a reference to it bursting during the siege. Indeed it may be to this bombardment that we owe the heap of stone cannon balls to be seen on the floor of the gatehouse, and to their battering that we should ascribe the loss of most of the outer curtain wall along the east and south sides of the castle. Few details have come down to us of Harlech's recapture by Harry of Monmouth, prince of Wales — the future King Henry V (1413–22) and victor of Agincourt — but according to one chronicler the prince's contemporary siege of Glyn Dŵr's garrison at Aberystwyth was conducted *'by mynes and all manner of engins that were thought needful for the distruccion of them and of there castle'*. Harlech appears to have fallen in early February 1409, as much due to a lack of supplies and exhaustion as to the effect of cannon balls.

Above: A fifteenth-century cannon from Cardiff Castle of the type that may have been used in the English siege of Harlech Castle in 1408–09 (Cardiff City Council).

Right: As a result of the siege, most of the outer curtain along the east and south sides of the castle was destroyed.

Harlech in the Wars of the Roses

Sixty years later, Harlech was playing a prominent part in the Wars of the Roses (1455–85). In the summer of 1460 it gave shelter to Queen Margaret of Anjou (d. 1482), the wife of King Henry VI (1422–61, 1470–71), and in 1461–68 it was held for the Lancastrians by a Welsh constable, Dafydd ab Ieuan ab Einion. After almost a decade as a thorn in the side of the Yorkist faction, in 1468 King Edward IV (1461–70, 1471–83) determined upon the necessity of capturing this stubborn outpost of Lancastrian resistance. 'Kyng Edward', wrote the chronicler John Warkworth, 'was possessed of alle Englonde, excepte a castelle in Northe Wales called Harlake, which Sere Richard Tunstall kepte, the qwiche was gotene afterwards by the Lord Harberde'.

In fact, the king empowered Lord William Herbert (d. 1469) of Raglan, Lord Harberde, to raise a substantial force, variously estimated at between 7,000 and 10,000 men. Herbert and his brother, Sir Richard Herbert (d. 1469), marched northwards with two wings of their great army converging on Harlech. The ensuing siege was graphically described by the poet, Hywel Dafi, who told of men being 'shattered by the sound of guns', with 'seven thousand men shooting in every port, their bows made from every yew tree'. The Lancastrian defenders held out for less than a month, surrendering the castle on 14 August. Fifty prisoners were taken, including Dafydd ab Ieuan ab Einion who had kept 'little Harlech for so long, alone faithful to the weak crown'.

It was the Yorkist siege of 1468 which is traditionally supposed to have given rise to the well-known song, Men of Harlech.

The Sixteenth Century

There is no record that the castle was repaired after the Glyn Dŵr sieges. When we next hear of Harlech, in 1539, it is in a report of Crown surveyors who declared that Conwy, Caernarfon and Harlech were all wholly unfurnished with means of defence and — in the event of invasion by the French or the Scots — incapable of being

William Herbert of Raglan (d. 1469) kneels at the feet of his patron, King Edward IV (1461–70, 1471–83), in this manuscript illumination of about 1461–62 (British Library, Royal Ms. 18 D II, f. 6).

In 1468, Lord William Herbert of Raglan, later earl of Pembroke, led an army of up to 10,000 men against the Lancastrian forces at Harlech; the ensuing siege lasted for less than a month. This near-contemporary manuscript illumination shows a siege of the period with guns, an assault tower and bowmen (British Library, Royal Ms. 14 E IV, f. 281 v).

John Speed's plan of the castle and town at Harlech dates from 1610. A contemporary description of the borough refers to 'a verye poore towne … having no traphicke or trade' (National Library of Wales).

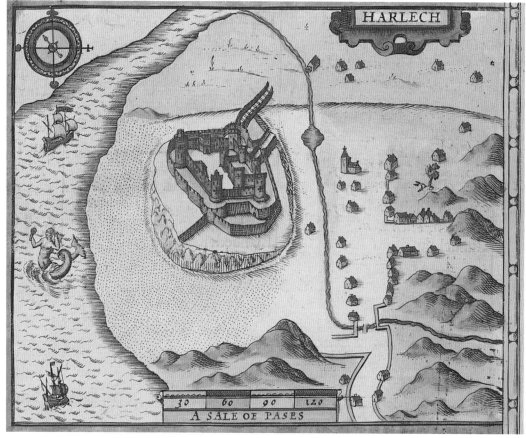

As with all of Edward I's major castles in north Wales, the stronghold at Harlech was accompanied by a new town. The infant borough received its royal charter in 1284, though the settlement never grew to any great size. This common seal of the borough dates to 1549: *SIGILLV':COMMVN':DE: HARDLECH (Society of Antiquaries).*

defended one hour. Another survey, of 1564, reported the interior of nearly every tower in the castle to be 'in utter ruin', the hall and chapel were roofless and the other buildings in the courtyard 'utterlie in ruyn and prostrate'. The place of the drawbridges was taken by makeshift constructions of timber and planks, themselves 'in greate decaye'.

In the reign of Queen Elizabeth I (1558–1603) it was directed that the Merioneth Assizes be held at Harlech and, for this purpose, at least the principal rooms in the gatehouse must have been maintained in occupiable condition. A paper of 1604 sets out the arguments 'for the keeping of the Sessions, etc., at Harlech', rather than at Bala where the justices preferred.

The paper points out that the castle is: 'as yet kept in somme better reparacion than anye of his Majesty's Castles in North Walles by reason that the Justices of the Assize, Sheriffe and Plenotarye, with there trayne, doe vse, when the assises are kepte in that Towne, to lie and keepe their diet within the said Castle. At which tyme the said Castle is aired, scowred, cleansed, and

some charges bestowed by every Sheriffe towards the reparacion thereof at every time they doe vse to resort thither to keepe the Sessions. If the Justices had not resorted to it, the Castle had been quite ruinated and decayed, but if the Sessions continue the Castle will be kept in reparacion without charge to His Majesty'.

It is stated that the: 'common gayle of the Castle is usually kept in the said Towne, and the poor prisoners therin relieved by the inhabitants thereof … , but the Justices now, respecting ther owne ease more than the good of the towne and ease of the countery, doe most commonlie vse to keepe their sessions at Bala, being a very fylthie dyrtie towne, without any lodgings fitt for gentlemen to lie, and a place farre remote and very vnconvenient for any general mytings'.

It is shown that it is very necessary that the Castle: 'standinge upon the sea side, with havnes of both sides, be maintained and kepte in reparaccion, so that his majestie may easilie (if need be) fortifie the same — as well as keepe the Countery in awe from anye insurrection, or rebellion, as alsoe to resist and withstand foraine powers'.

The Civil War and After

Forty years later, many of the medieval castles of England and Wales saw a last brief phase of military activity in the Civil War of 1642–48. Some of them, such as Donnington in Berkshire, Old Basing in Hampshire, or Denbigh and Raglan in Wales, were subjected, sometimes more than once, to protracted siege and bombardment. From the spring of 1644, Harlech was defended for the king by its constable, Colonel William Owen (d. 1670) of Brogyntyn. The castle seems to have been under siege by a parliamentary force from late June 1646. When the surviving garrison of 16 officers, gentlemen and invalids, together with 28 common soldiers, finally surrendered to Major-General Thomas Mytton (d. 1656) on 15 March 1647, Harlech was the last royalist stronghold of all to be lost. Its fall signified the end of the Civil War.

The parliamentarians are said to have rendered the castle untenable and to have destroyed the two gatehouse staircases (both renewed in modern times). Fortunately, an order to demolish it was not proceeded with, and though bereft of its floors and its roofs, its glass and its wood and its lead, its main structure still stands very largely complete, as striking a monument as any of its north Wales contemporaries to the skill and art of the

castle-builders who conceived and created it towards the close of the thirteenth century.

From the eighteenth century, the castle began to attract the interest of topographical artists. The earliest depiction is the engraving by the brothers Samuel and Nathaniel Buck, published in 1742. When the travelling writer Thomas Pennant saw Harlech in 1770 he described it as 'a small and very poor town, remarkable only for its castle,

Above: Major-General Thomas Mytton (d. 1656), from England's Worthies ... *by John Vicars (London 1647). In May 1645, Mytton became the parliamentary commander in north Wales. The garrison at Harlech surrendered to the major-general on 15 March 1647 (British Library).*

Left: From the spring of 1644, William Owen (d. 1670) acted as the king's commander at Harlech (National Library of Wales).

THE NORTH WEST VIEW OF HARLECH CASTLE, IN THE COUNTY OF MERIONETH.

Following the Civil War siege of 1646–47, the castle was said to have been rendered untenable, though an order for total demolition was not carried through. This 1742 engraving by Samuel and Nathaniel Buck shows the castle still standing very largely complete (National Library of Wales).

Right: Paul Sandby (1731–1809) was one of many artists drawn to Harlech in the eighteenth and nineteenth centuries by the Picturesque qualities of the site. His aquatint of 1776 shows the stronghold from the foot of the castle rock, looking northwards 'with Snowdon at a distance' (Leeds Museums and Galleries, City Art Gallery).

which is seated on a lofty rock ... a noble square building'. In the late eighteenth century, and on into the nineteenth century, it was the superb Picturesque qualities of the site which continued to attract the attention of artists such as Paul Sandby (1731–1809), J. M. W. Turner (1775–1851), John Varley (1778–1842), John Sell Cotman (1782–1842) and Henry Gastineau (1791–1876).

Harlech has always remained a property of the Crown. Until transferred to the Office of Works in 1914, responsibility for its care — as part of the Merioneth Crown Estate — lay with the Office of Woods and Forests, who carried out many useful repairs, including the renewal of the arches over the entrance passage through the gatehouse. The general overhaul of the stonework, together with the excavation of the main ward and exposure of wall foundations to original levels was carried out under the direction of Sir Charles Peers (1868–1952) during the years following the end of the 1914–18 war. In 1969 ancient monuments in Wales became the responsibility of the Welsh Office, and the castle is now maintained on behalf of the National Assembly for Wales by Cadw: Welsh Historic Monuments.

In 1987, Harlech Castle — together with Beaumaris Castle, Caernarfon Castle and town walls, and Conwy Castle and town walls — was inscribed on the World Heritage List as an historic site of outstanding universal value.

In 1914, responsibility for the care of Harlech passed to the Office of Works. A general overhaul and consolidation of the stonework was to follow the 1914–18 war. This view shows work in progress on the gatehouse in 1922.

A Tour of Harlech Castle

Siting and Plan

Even in the context of such rivals as Conwy, Caernarfon and Beaumaris, Harlech is scenically perhaps the most sublime of all the north Wales castles. Its rugged rock-based walls and towers achieve a serene and abiding harmony with the nearby hills and distant heights. No visitor who can spare the time should miss the reality of the well-known view of the castle from the south, with Snowdon's peak as the climax to the backcloth of mountain summits, and with the flat green lands of the *morfa* running out to the sandhills and the silver sea at the panorama's western edge. The viewpoint for this lies just south of the town, on an open rocky knoll beside the Barmouth road.

The castle is splendidly sited on a bold and rugged promontory, rising barely 200 feet (60m) above sea level. This headland of rock is a spur of the Harlech Dome, a famous geological feature comprising a hard, tough grit or sandstone belonging to the lower part of the Cambrian system. Jutting out towards the sea, and falling away steeply on all sides except the east, the site has great natural military strength. It provided the ideal platform for the architectural masterpiece that Edward I's builders erected on it.

The castle proper occupies a levelled area towards the south side of the headland. The inner ward, which is the heart of the castle, forms a quadrangle surrounded by curtain walls. On the east and west sides, these walls are parallel, but to the north and south they splay outwards to accommodate the great gatehouse. The gatehouse itself dominates the whole group of buildings from a position astride the centre of the eastern curtain. A lower and slighter outer curtain wall closely envelops the inner ring of walls, gatehouse and four corner towers. This provides for a concentric, but somewhat narrow and constricted, outer ward.

The only directions from which a land-based attack could conceivably be mounted on the castle were to the east and south. On these two sides, a deep and wide rock-cut ditch was set out in a further concentric line to the outer ward. This ditch was never intended to be water-filled; its scale alone was enough of an obstacle to mining or the bringing up of siege engines.

Beyond the heart of the castle, a large enclosed area of rock extends to the north and is bounded by a ravine and a waterfall. And to the west, the face of the headland falls away precipitously to sea level. Here, at the foot of the castle, was a water gate. How near the seashore came up to this gate in the thirteenth century is not known with any certainty, but a channel must have been made to allow ships to approach it and unload. A path from the water gate up to the castle is ledged against the overhanging rock, and is protected from above by two 'artillery' platforms which still survive.

Opposite: Harlech stands on a bold and rugged promontory of rock, jutting out towards Tremadog Bay. The site was to provide an ideal platform for the architectural masterpiece designed and built by King Edward I's military engineers led by Master James of St George (Skyscan Balloon Photography for Cadw).

The symmetry and imposing strength of the defences are particularly apparent from the eastern — landward — approach to the castle.

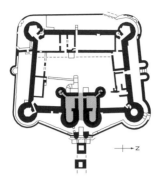

Opposite: The magnificent façade of the east gatehouse presents an image of uncompromising power and impregnability towards the most likely direction of attack. The numbers highlight those features described in the text.

The Gatehouse

Today, most visitors approach the castle down the short hill from High Street and enter it from the east or main gate. Seen from the car park, only the ditch bridge towers, much of the low outer curtain wall, and the high battlements are wanting. What remains continues to convey an overwhelming sense of symmetry in design. It presents an image of uncompromising power and impregnability towards the only possible direction of attack.

From the ticket office, a modern timber bridge and steps lead up towards the main gate. Behind the ticket office, the children's playing field is on the site of the filled-in castle pond. Before climbing up to the main gate it is well worth pausing to consider some of the exterior details.

External Features

Looking at the gatehouse, in the centre you should note the lancet window of the lower chapel [1], with a large formerly-grilled window in the towers to either side [2]. Above you will see the corresponding window arrangement of the chapel [3] and flanking rooms of the top floor [4]. Above again there is a chamfered stringcourse [5], here surviving complete and binding the whole architectural composition together. It also marks the base of the battlemented parapet in which one whole arrowloop and several bases still remain [6]. On the left-hand tower only,

there is a great sweeping slope of six putlog holes of the helicoidal or spiral scaffolding used by the original builders [7]. Notice also how the solid turrets [8] of the outer gate are pushing forward in front of the inner towers in a commanding salient. These turrets are corbelled out to rise from a smooth sloping apron of stone, itself rising sheer from the rock-cut edge of the deep eastern ditch. You will see how the remains of the outer curtain [9], battered down in one or other of the castle's sieges, fall away to left and right of the gate turrets. The height and now lost battlementing of this outer curtain would originally have been maintained all round the great outer bastions or mantelets at the south-east and north-east angles and along the south and north sides.

You are now ready to enter the heart of the castle, and should ascend the modern timber staircase beside and above the foundations of the two early fourteenth-century bridge towers.

At the top of the staircase, you will be standing at the point where an inner drawbridge pivoted to come down against the nearer of the bridge towers. Looking back, you must envisage an elevated passage leading into the castle at this level. It ran through arches in both of the bridge towers, and was supported on a stone-arched centre bridge (see reconstruction p. 8). The whole arrangement continued on towards the main gate-passage, through which access is still gained to the inner ward.

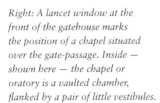

Right: A lancet window at the front of the gatehouse marks the position of a chapel situated over the gate-passage. Inside — shown here — the chapel or oratory is a vaulted chamber, flanked by a pair of little vestibules.

Far right: Mass in the small chapels in the gatehouse would have been said in private for the constable, his family and visiting dignitaries. In this manuscript illumination a royal lady holds back her curtain of privacy as a priest raises the Eucharist (British Library, Yates Thompson Ms. 13, f. 7).

The Main Gate-Passage

Having passed through the outer gate, we come
to the principal entry to the inside of the castle.
This, the main gate-passage, is itself worth careful
inspection. It housed a succession of obstacles,
and each section of the passage could be used to
isolate and detain any would-be entrant by closing
a barrier behind him before opening the one in
front. Indications of all these barriers are still visible.

To begin with, outside the first arch, a two-leaved
wooden door opened outwards against the flat sides
of the flanking towers, shaped for this purpose. The
doors were secured by a heavy drawbar, the hole for
which can be seen running into the thickness
of the wall on the left, immediately inside the arch.
Behind the doors, just in front of the next arch, there
was a heavy portcullis, the grooves for which remain
intact. There were arrowloops from the guardrooms
on either side, covering an entrant as he moved
forward towards the next barrier. This was a second
portcullis, situated in front of the next arch, and
beyond this was a second two-leaved door opening
inwards, with the hole for the sliding drawbar again
visible. Then comes the main length of the passage,
at the end of which doorways on either side lead
through to flanking porters' rooms. From these
rooms, winding stairs lead up to the residential
apartments above. Overhead, you will see the
springers of three intermediate unrestored arches
which carried the floor of the room over the
passage. Beyond the two side doorways are the
grooves for a third portcullis barring entry to the
courtyard, and in front of this there was possibly a
third two-leaved door opening inwards, but all
evidence for this has now gone.

Look up into the narrow space between the
last two arches and you will see, through a square
opening in what is the window seat of the room
above, a small hole situated in the ceiling of the
window embrasure. A pulley wheel was suspended
at this point, carrying the rope or chain used to
raise and lower the portcullis. Similar evidence is
also detectable above the other two portcullises.

The Gatehouse Guardrooms

On the left (south) of the gate-passage you will find
a single ground-floor room (currently housing an
exhibition). There is a wide arch across the centre of
this chamber, but there is no evidence for a fireplace
and its precise use is uncertain. The doorway in the
south-west corner gives access to one of the stairs
leading to the upper levels of the building. At the
far end of the room (beyond the exhibition), the
hole for the drawbar securing the outermost doors
of the gate-passage comes right through the wall.
Clearly, this was the point from which the outer
doors were controlled.

Glancing up through the floorless interior,
you will gain some impression of the layout and
pattern of the upper levels. On both floors, the
space above the gate-passage and this southern
guardroom was divided into two rooms. Towards

*Any would-be entrant to the
inner ward of the castle had
to pass through a succession
of obstacles situated along
the length of the main gate-
passage. Indications of all
these barriers are still visible
with careful observation.*

Above: Fireplaces were fitted in each of the four rooms located on the two upper floors at the southern side of the gatehouse. The flues of these fireplaces rise within the walls and meet at the remains of an impressive group of linked chimneys above roof level.

Left: Cutaway reconstruction of the gate-passage (Chris Jones-Jenkins, 1986).

the inner ward courtyard, the larger and grander room at each level was fitted with two tall, stately window embrasures. Each of the two forward rooms was lit by a pair of smaller windows. All four rooms were fitted with fireplaces, with those in the large rooms facing the courtyard being particularly fine examples. The flues of these fireplaces rise to an impressive group of linked chimneys, of which a considerable fragment remains visible above roof level.

To the right of the passage are two ground-floor rooms with a communicating door. The first room, with a fireplace and lighting loops both to north and west, must have served as the porter's lodge. In the north-west corner is a door to staircase communication with the upper levels. As has been earlier suggested (p. 10), the stone cannon balls now collected in this room may bear witness to the cannonading suffered by the castle in one of the fifteenth-century sieges. As on the other side of the passage, one's eye is drawn up through the site of vanished floors and ceilings to the stately window openings and hooded chimney pieces of the rooms above.

Sir John de Bonvillars

Sir John de Bonvillars was one of the distinguished Savoyard knights in the household of King Edward I. He was appointed deputy justiciar of north Wales and appears to have played a significant role in the king's castle-building operations between 1283 and 1287. In 1285 he was appointed constable of Harlech Castle at an annual fee of £149. It seems likely that the first-floor apartment in the gatehouse was quickly made ready to receive Sir John and his wife, Agnes, in the closing months of 1285.

Sir John died in the king's service at the siege of Dryslwyn Castle in August 1287. Agnes, his widow, assumed the constable's responsibilities at Harlech and presumably continued to occupy the same gatehouse apartment until 1290.

The seal of Sir John de Bonvillars (d. 1287), constable of Harlech Castle 1285–87. The original is attached to a deed dated at Evian, Savoy, in 1279 (Archivio di Stato, Torino, Baronia di Vaud 27, Mezières, documento n. 1).

Remainder of the Gatehouse

You may now wish to cross over to the far side of the courtyard and sit in one of the window seats to look back at a general view of the main inward façade of the gatehouse. It is undoubtedly one of the most striking compositions of 'military' (or perhaps more accurately 'fortified domestic') architecture of the thirteenth century to be seen anywhere in Britain.

Notice in particular that the six great windows (three to each floor) have all been reduced in height, probably at some early point in their history. You will see that their originally traceried heads are filled-in beneath the relieving arches with solid blocks of squared stone. It is interesting to note the way these grand openings contrast functionally with the pleasant irregularity of the little slits that light the stairs, at varying levels, in the two corner turrets. Hidden behind the turrets, as we shall see later, there is an additional grand window situated at either end of the top floor. These are visible from the wall-walk, and each retains fragments of its thirteenth-century stone tracery. Taken together, there is sufficient evidence to allow a reliable reconstruction of the original form of all eight windows.

Note also the wide external staircase — 'a stately stayre' as it is called in one of the sixteenth-century surveys — which leads up from the courtyard to a door at first-floor level. This door enabled direct communication to be maintained at all times between the constable's lodging and the rest of the castle, even when the formidable barriers of the gate-passage were all closed, as generally they all were.

Now let us return across the courtyard and ascend this stair to the viewing platform provided in the doorway. From here you will see almost all of the arrangements in the two upper floors of the gatehouse. In effect, the four principal rooms at each level comprised a self-contained apartment (see plan, p. 25). To your right, in each case, there was a great chamber or hall [1] fitted with a handsome fireplace [2]. Indeed, the fireplace on the first floor may well have been 'the chimney in the chamber of Sir John Bonvillars', for the making of which Master Peter Morel and Albert de Menz — masons — were paid 7s. 6d. in January 1286. Both floors had two generous windows [3] towards the courtyard and another in the end wall [4]. A doorway in the south-west corner [5] of the chambers communicated with the southern

Opposite: The inner façade of the gatehouse undoubtedly represents one of the most striking compositions of thirteenth-century 'fortified domestic' architecture to be seen anywhere in the British Isles.

Originally, there was a traceried-stone head in each of the six grand windows at the back of the gatehouse. More evidence for the form of the tracery survives in the single window at either end of the upper floor. Here, the southern example is shown.

Taken together, there is enough evidence to allow a reliable reconstruction of the form of all eight grand windows at the back of the gatehouse. The heads were glazed and the lower parts fitted with wooden shutters only (Illustration by Chris Jones-Jenkins, 1996).

There is a striking resemblance between the dimensions of the Harlech gatehouse windows and those of a similar design at the Savoy castle of Chillon (Switzerland). Both sets of windows appear to derive from a common pattern book (Peter Humphries).

In this cutaway reconstruction through the gatehouse, the northern half of the structure has been reduced to ground level. Details of the gate-passage and the floors to the south have been restored. The battlements are shown surmounted with stone pinnacles, a feature seen at Conwy Castle and one linked to the Savoy connections of Master James of St George. Although not conclusive, slight evidence for pinnacles has also been traced at Harlech (Illustration by Chris Jones-Jenkins, 1996).

staircase. Another doorway in the opposite corner [**6**] led to the smaller chamber at the front of the gatehouse [**7**]. This same doorway also gave access to adjacent latrines, contained within the thickness of the walls [**8**]. Finally, directly ahead of the viewing platform, a third doorway [**9**] led into a small oratory or chapel, located over the front of the gate-passage, between the projecting east towers. At each level, the chapel was flanked by a pair of little vestibules or vestries.

To the left of the viewing platform, looking through the doorway, you will see a smaller room or chamber on both floors [**10**]. Each has a fireplace [**11**], and there is a single window towards the courtyard [**12**] and another in the north end wall [**13**]. In the north-west corner, a door [**14**] communicated with the north staircase. Once again, in the opposite corner, another door [**15**] led to the room at the front of the gatehouse [**16**] and — in the thickness of the wall — to an adjacent latrine [**17**].

In each floor level, the larger and smaller western rooms, or the hall and chamber of each apartment [**1** and **10**], were living rooms. By elimination, the rooms adjoining them in the eastern towers [**7** and **16**] would have been bedchambers. One must assume that the lower suite, with its direct access to the courtyard and its control of the three portcullises, was the apartment of the constable and his family. He was the king's lieutenant and commandant of the castle and its garrison. The upper suite, one may suppose, but with more caution, may have been intended for the accommodation of visiting dignitaries — the king, the prince, the justiciar, the chamberlain of north Wales, or perhaps the sheriff of Merioneth.

First-Floor Plan of the Gatehouse

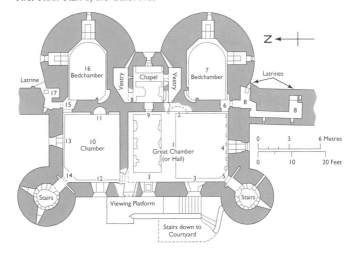

Each of the great chambers on the southern side of the gatehouse was fitted with a handsome hooded fireplace.

The Inner Ward

Next we shall consider the four towers of the inner ward in turn. For ease of description they are here named from the points of the compass as the north-east, south-east, south-west, and north-west towers. A survey of 1343 names them as the Prison, Garden, Weathercock and Chapel towers respectively, while a sixteenth-century survey names them as the Debtors', Mortimer, Bronwen and Armourer's towers. Let us begin with the two eastern towers — the 'towers towards the town' — which belong to the initial building period, and each of which contains a staircase giving access from ground to wall-walk level and down again.

North-East Tower

The tower is entered from the corner of the courtyard to the north of the gatehouse. A reconstructed newel stair leads directly up to first-floor level, where a small lobby, with an opening off to a latrine, precedes the main room. The room itself has a corner fireplace and two formerly heavily barred window openings, once closed by internal shutters of which one of the hinges still remains. The floor of the room is now missing, but it contained a trapdoor which was the only means of entry to the deep circular dungeon below. The dungeon's only vent for light and air was a narrow slit sloping steeply up through the thickness of the wall. The second-floor room also has a corner fireplace, and both rooms are seven-sided.

The stair continues up to the wall-walk, passing a small latrine at the top. When you emerge on the wall-walk, you should turn to your left and follow the north-eastern wall as far as the gatehouse. Here you will see two doorways: one originally communicated between the gate and the wall-top; the second led from the gate to an adjacent latrine. To the right, you will see a traceried window remaining to full height.

Now you should retrace your steps and walk right around the wall-tops to the southern side of the gatehouse. From here there is a good view of the corresponding traceried window; this one lighting the great chamber on the top floor. Notice, too, the refashioned slate roof covering the latrine projection.

From here, you should descend back to the courtyard by way of the newel stair in the south-east tower.

South-East Tower

The arrangement of this tower closely parallels that already noted in the north-east tower. There are again three levels, with two seven-sided rooms with corner fireplaces surmounting a circular dungeon-like basement. The basement has only a narrow slit shaft for light and air, sloping up through the thickness of the wall to emerge just below a first-floor window.

Having arrived back at ground level, cross the courtyard to the western towers which were built in 1288–89.

South-West Tower and North-West Tower

A Master William of Drogheda was paid for the making of these two towers and their turrets in 1289. For the southern tower, which was 52 feet (15.8m) high, he received £117 at the task rate of 45s. per foot. For the northern tower, which reached 49 1/2 feet (15.1m) in height, Master William's payment amounted to £111 7s. 6d., again at the rate of 45s. per foot. William was also paid £11 8s. for each of the turrets, both of which were 19 feet (5.8m) high, at a rate of 12s. per foot.

From this same year, we also have a record of £6 5s. being paid for dressing a total of 171 stone corbels. These were intended to support the turret parapets on the two western towers, and also to support the parapets of the two gatehouse stair turrets. Thirty-three of the corbels were dressed at a rate of 1s. each, and the other 138 at 8d. each; all of them are still in position today.

Each of the western towers contains four five-sided rooms, of which the two middle rooms in each case are provided with fireplaces. Doorways in the corners of the courtyard lead into each tower. In both of them the floors are missing and the staircases

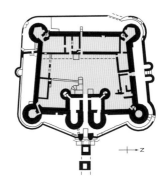

Opposite: Master William of Drogheda was paid for the construction of the north-west tower in 1289. He worked at the task rate of 45s. per foot on a tower which reached almost 50 feet (15.2m) high. Master William received a further £11 8s. for the turret at the rate of 12s. per foot. Two more masons, Nicholas of Newingham and Ralf of Radwell, dressed the corbels intended to support the turret parapets.

Former Names of the Castle Towers

Modern Name	Survey of 1343 or Earlier	Survey of 1564
North-East Tower	Le Prisontour (also in 1321)	Debtors' Tower
South-East Tower	Turris Ultra Gardinum (i.e. Garden Tower)	Mortimer Tower
South-West Tower	Le Wedercoktour	Bronwen Tower
North-West Tower	Le Chapeltour	Armourer's Tower
Gatehouse	Le Gemeltour Supra Portam (i.e. Twin Tower Over the Gate)	

Little survives of the range of buildings located along the northern side of the courtyard. Here, the chapel is the most prominent feature. The numbers highlight those features described in the text.

ruined and inaccessible, so that it is now only possible to inspect the interiors from below. If the name 'Armourer's Tower', used for the north-west tower in the sixteenth century, was traditional, it may be that this tower contained the workshop of the 'artiller' mentioned in the original garrison establishment of 1284.

The North Range

The positions of the various buildings situated around the edges of the inner ward courtyard are marked on the plan (inside back cover). For the most part their remains are fragmentary, and to view them it is suggested that you should stand in the centre of the courtyard. Beginning with the northern side, to the left there is an open yard leading into the north-west tower [1]. Next to this is the castle chapel [2], with its east and west walls remaining to full height. Corbels [3], beam-holes [4] and a

stringcourse [5] on the north curtain, and the terminating line of white internal plastering on its west wall indicate the position of the chapel's inner ceiling and its outer lean-to roof. Opposite the traces of plastering, there still survives the lancet head of the east window. The moulded bases of the chapel door jambs remain near the south-west corner [6].

To the east of the chapel, there is a gateway communicating with the outer ward, and thence through the outer north gate with the castle rock. Next again, to the right, are three windows [7–9] that lighted a group of service buildings, in one of which may still be seen the castle well [10]. Beam-holes in the wall above [11] indicate the height of their lean-to roof. Notice also on the north curtain wall a line of eight small holes [12] sloping up from left to right. These are putlog holes of the sloped scaffolding used in the original building works of the 1280s.

The Savoy Connection with Harlech

The boundaries of the historic princedom of Savoy embraced an alpine region in what is today part of south-eastern France, western Switzerland, and north-west Italy. In the thirteenth century, the ruling dynasty of Savoy was of great importance. King Edward had close family ties with the dominion, and he was familiar with Savoyards who had come to England during his father's reign. Edward's visit to Savoy in 1273 provided an opportunity to renew these dynastic links. During his reign, there were many Savoyards among his close friends and the servants of the royal household.

Edward was eventually to engage the Savoy master mason, James of St George, as his chief military architect (p. 7). Other Savoyard craftsmen also worked on the construction of his north Wales castles. It is, therefore, perhaps not surprising to find several distinct architectural details which occur both in Savoy and north Wales, but which are rarely encountered elsewhere. Indeed, at Harlech there is evidence for all the main architectural links:

- The use of helicoidal or inclined scaffolding, as on the south tower of the gatehouse.
- The use of round-headed arches, with that between the solid turrets of the outer gate being a particularly good example.
- A distinct form of latrine shaft with a marked similarity between the corbelled turret at Harlech and those to be seen at La Bâtiaz (Valais).
- A common window design, with those in the gatehouse at Harlech (p. 23) bearing a striking resemblance to examples at Chillon (Switzerland).
- Evidence for the embellishment of the castle battlements by triplets of stone pinnacles, as at Conwy (p. 24).

Above: A semi-circular gate arch at the Porte du Sex in the town wall at Saillon in Switzerland. The gate can be firmly dated to 1257–58 (Peter Humphries).

Below: The arch in the outer gate at Harlech bears a close resemblance to that at Saillon.

Far left: Corbelled latrine turrets on the north-west curtain wall at the castle of La Bâtiaz (Valais) in Switzerland (Peter Humphries).

Left: A similar turret on the south wall of the outer ward at Harlech.

The range of buildings along the west side of the courtyard included the hall (to the right of this view) and the castle kitchens (to the far left). In the hall, there are four windows looking out towards the sea, with a fireplace at the centre.

The West Range

If you now turn to look at the west side of the courtyard, on the right is the site of the great hall. It has four window openings towards the sea and there is a fireplace between them. The inner wall of the hall is now almost wholly demolished, though the gable wall at its northern end still stands to full height. A series of beam-holes and corbels, a dripstone and flashing groove along the outer wall mark the position of its inner and outer roofs.

To the left is the kitchen area, separated from the hall by a passage and the site of the buttery and pantry. A substantial fragment of the kitchen's inner wall still stands, and on it are three massive corbels below a dripstone. Together these indicate the position of the pent-roof covering a passage which appears to have run the length of the buildings on this side of the courtyard.

The South Range

Against the southern curtain are the footings of two buildings. That to the left is traditionally identified as the granary, with floor beam-holes in the curtain wall indicating that it was built over a low basement. To the right is the site of a room which may represent the *Styngwernehalle* mentioned in the survey of 1343, presumably a Welsh timber-framed hall dismantled and brought here at the time of the building of the castle from a nearby place named Ystumgwern. On the curtain wall above, to left and right, note the lines of putlog holes of two sloping scaffold ramps, less easily picked out than those on the curtain opposite. Notice also, to the left, how the full thickness of the eastern curtain, apparently never completed, terminates on a sloping line some way below the finished top of the main wall.

The Outer Ward

The outer ward, which closely encircles the curtains and towers of the inner ward on all four sides, provides the best viewing points for noting a number of features of interest. First, the horizontal constructional breaks mentioned above (pp. 6–7) are clearly visible about 15 feet (4.5m) above the ground along the whole length of both the north and south curtains. On the west, the vertical breaks can also be seen in the sides of some of the seaward-facing window openings.

Walking around, you will also notice, on the dressings of most of the larger external windows at first-floor level, the marks of the iron grilles that formerly barred them. Lines of sloping putlog holes indicating the use of helicoidal scaffolding are prominent on the south tower of the gatehouse and the north-east tower, and especially so at all levels of the south-west tower. The bases, at alternating heights, of a number of the arrowloops of the destroyed outer curtain may be seen in what still remains of it on both the south and east sides. Notable also on the south side is the curve of the great projecting latrine and rubbish chute. Here, too, the depth of the rock-cut ditch is particularly impressive.

The 'Way from the Sea'

The 'way from the sea' can best be seen by descending to and returning from the water gate at the foot of the castle rock near the railway station. The outward front of the water gate is no longer intact, though you will be able to make out the pit of a former drawbridge, and there is some evidence that the nearby rock was faced with stone to form a glacis (similar to the wall beside the water gate at Rhuddlan Castle). The wall encircling the castle rock makes an indent here, and this may relate to the former presence of a dock immediately outside the gateway.

From the water gate, 108 shallow steps lead up to an intermediate turret, where a fixed wooden ramp now occupies the position of a former drawbridge. The bridge and its turret are skilfully sited in an awkward re-entrant of the rock, where the south-west tower of the castle itself towers menacingly above them. From this 'upper gate' a further flight of 19 steps leads up to the grassy area below the south-west mantelet, from which there is a fine view of the south ditch, the south curtains (inner and outer) and the semi-circular latrine projection. The path leads on up to a gate at the foot of the north-west tower.

The parapet wall that protected the 'way' ends in the remains of a small gated turret against the side of the south-west mantelet,

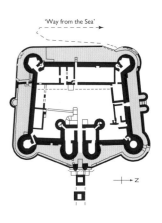

The 'way from the sea' snakes down the western side of the castle rock from the outer ward via the upper gate to the water gate.

whence a short flight of steps would have led down into the south ditch, which at this point fell sheer into the south-west ravine. The whole drama is lost today, the ravine being effectively blocked from view by a spinney of sturdy sycamores growing in it.

In this short description of the castle it is hoped the visitor's attention will have been drawn to the main features of interest. No written description, however full, can convey the whole grandeur of Harlech as an outstanding monument of medieval military architecture, nearly as impressive and in essentials nearly as complete as when it was built more than seven centuries ago.

Although now isolated from the sea, Harlech Castle still dominates the coastal landscape, overlooking the morfa *and sandhills which stretch out into Tremadog Bay.*

Further Reading

R. R. Davies, *Conquest, Coexistence, and Change: Wales 1063–1415* (Oxford 1987); reprinted in paperback as, *The Age of Conquest: Wales 1063–1415* (Oxford 1991).

R. R. Davies, *The Revolt of Owain Glyn Dŵr* (Oxford 1995).

J. Goronwy Edwards, 'Edward I's Castle-Building in Wales', *Proceedings of the British Academy*, **32** (1946), 15–81.

Harold Hughes, 'Harlech Castle', *Archaeologia Cambrensis*, sixth series, **13** (1913), 275–316.

E. Neaverson, *Mediaeval Castles in North Wales: A Study of Sites, Water Supply and Building Stones* (Liverpool and London 1947), 48–49.

C. R. Peers, 'Harlech Castle', *Transactions of the Honourable Society of Cymmrodorion* (1921–22), 63–82.

A. J. Taylor, 'Harlech Castle: The Dating of the Outer Enclosure', *Journal of the Merioneth Historical and Record Society*, **I** (1949–51), 202–3.

A. J. Taylor, 'Some Notes on the Savoyards in North Wales, 1277–1300, with Special Reference to the Savoyard Element in the Construction of Harlech Castle', *Genava*, new series, **2** (Genève 1963), 289–315.

A. J. Taylor, 'Who was "John Pennardd, Leader of the Men of Gwynedd"?', *English Historical Review*, **91** (1976), 79–97.

A. J. Taylor, 'Castle-Building in Thirteenth-Century Wales and Savoy', *Proceedings of the British Academy*, **63** (1977), 265–92.

Arnold Taylor, *The Welsh Castles of Edward I* (London 1986).

Glanmor Williams, *Recovery, Reorientation and Reformation: Wales c. 1415–1642* (Oxford 1987); reprinted in paperback as *Renewal and Reformation: Wales c. 1415–1642* (Oxford 1993).